YOU CAN'T SNEEZE
WITH YOUR EYES OPEN
& Other Freaky Facts About the Human Body

for Heather,
who has the gift of laughter

YOU CAN'T SNEEZE
WITH YOUR EYES OPEN

& Other Freaky Facts
About the Human Body

BARBARA SEULING
Illustrated by Jeremy Tapscott

KNIGHT BOOKS
Hodder and Stoughton

Printed and bound in Great Britain
for Hodder and Stoughton Chil-
dren's Books, a division of Hodder
and Stoughton Ltd., Mill Road,
Dunton Green, Sevenoaks, Kent
TN13 2YA. (Editorial Office: 47
Bedford Square, London
WC1B 3DP) by Clays Ltd, St Ives plc.
Typeset by Rowland Phototypeset-
ting Ltd, Bury St Edmunds, Suffolk.

British Library C.I.P.
Seuling, Barbara
  You can't sneeze with eyes
  open: And other freaky facts
  about the human body.
  I. Title
  612

ISBN 0 340 54714 6

Contents

1

The Amazing Human Machine

☐ The queen of France, Catherine de Medicis, would not have a woman in her court with a waistline larger than 33 centimetres.

☐ Midget General Tom Thumb, 1.02 metres tall, a star of P. T. Barnum's circus, married teeny Lavinia Warren, 0.81 metres tall, on February 10, 1863, and at their wedding cut a cake that weighed more than they did.

☐ The tallest person ever recorded, 2.72 metres Robert Wadlow, was already 1.62 metres tall at the age of five, and was still growing at the time of his death at the age of twenty-two.

☐ William Howard Taft, twenty-seventh president of the United States, weighed over 136 kilos. He once got stuck in the White House bath and had to be removed with the help of others.

☐ People in the Canadian province of Quebec are approximately a size smaller than their fellow Canadians.

☐ When the architects of Lincoln Centre in New York City studied human dimensions for the installation of theatre seats, they discovered that the average American had grown considerably wider in the hips over the last fifty years.

☐ A law decreed by Benito Mussolini of Italy during World War II required a minimum height of 1.60 metres for government employees. Former Prime Minister Amintore Fanfani clearly broke the law in 1954, taking office while standing at a mere 1.55 metres, but President Sandro Pertini squeaked by legitimately – at a towering 1.60 metres.

☐ In Borneo, children were considered old enough to go to school if they could reach an arm over their heads and touch the opposite ear.

☐ Even bloodhounds and police dogs can't tell some identical twins apart.

☐ Between now and old age, you will walk about 70,000 miles.

☐ Showing or extending an open hand in greeting, as in a handshake, goes back to our earliest history. It indicates that we come in peace, carrying no weapons.

☐ In space, astronauts had to learn what to do with their bodies in a state of total weightlessness when they went to sleep. Soviet cosmonaut Gherman S. Titov had to tie his arms down with his belt because once he awoke to the alarming sight of his arms floating in mid-air.

☐ Unless you are rather unusual, you will spend about one-third of your life asleep. If, for any reason, you are continually deprived of sleep, you will probably have hallucinations and eventually go mad.

☐ Salvador Dali, the artist, devised his own alarm clock. He put a tin plate on the floor, then sat in a chair holding a spoon out over the plate. As he relaxed and slipped into a doze, the spoon went clattering to the floor, landing in the plate. The noise woke him up, and Dali went back to work.

☐ According to the prices listed in the catalogue of a bio-chemical company, the ingredients that make up a 45 kilo human being would be worth £1,846,420.

☐ We are not the first civilisation to consider disability income. Laws going back to the first Anglo-Danish king of Kent, Aethelbert, in A.D. 616, compensated a man for the loss of his fingers or thumb.

☐ A jogger's feet hit the ground about two thousand times in one mile. When you walk, your feet hit the ground about one thousand times in a mile.

☐ Tom Dempsey, born in 1947 with only half a foot, was encouraged by his father as he grew up to play sports and take part in all activities like the other kids. He did, and even excelled at them. He holds the NFL's record for the longest field goal – 57.60 metres.

☐ Grover Cleveland, twenty-second and twenty-fourth president of the United States, had an artificial jaw. The operation, done aboard a yacht in the Potomac, was kept a secret from the public for twenty-five years.

☐ Scientists believe that human beings of the future will have fewer teeth, no hair, and no little toes.

☐ A microchip may soon replace a part of the body that is no longer working. For example, an implanted chip controlled by a transistor or computer could restore sight to a blind person.

☐ Scientists are working on the principle of suspended animation so that astronauts of the future can sleep through long space flights without ageing, using very little food and oxygen. Short hops might include one to Uranus (16 years) or Neptune (30.7 years).

☐ Sleep-walking and sleep-talking often run in families.

☐ One out of every ten kids has probably had a sleep-walking experience.

☐ The human body can survive three minutes without oxygen, three days without water, and three weeks without food.

2

A Sound Foundation

☐ The hardest thing in the human body is tooth enamel.

☐ Your teeth started growing six months before you were born.

☐ Our gums are renewed at least twice each month.

☐ Toothache is more painful between 3 a.m. and dawn than at any other time.

☐ Foot sizes get larger with each generation.

☐ A broken bone in the leg or arm usually takes about twelve weeks to heal.

☐ The distance between the inside of your elbow and your wrist is approximately the same as the length of your foot.

So it is!

just ignore him and he might go away...

17

☐ Not all toes are created equal – your big toe has only two bones, while the rest have three.

☐ A karate expert can break a board with his bare hand because the bones of the hand compress in the collision. Bones can withstand greater compression than wood.

☐ Bone is very light, and full of tiny holes. Your skeleton accounts for only 14 per cent of your total body weight.

☐ Your skeleton does not hold up your body; it is the muscles and ligaments, not the bones, that hold your body upright.

☐ When a man bends at the waist to pick up 45 kilos, about 762 kilos of force is exerted on the disc between his last vertebra and his pelvis.

that's the last time I visit the petrified forest!

☐ When they were looking for a way to protect the heads of American football players, researchers studied the woodpecker because this bird hammers steadily with its head without suffering injury. A helmet was designed with air spaces similar to those in the woodpecker's skull, which act as shock absorbers.

☐ Your bone cells replace themselves in a rapid exchange, resulting in a brand-new skeleton about every two years.

☐ By the end of the day, a person has shrunk about two and a half centimetres – temporarily. The next morning, he's back to his old height again.

☐ A baby has a lot more bones than its father or mother. Dad, for example, has only one bone in his head – the skull – but his child has 29 separate bones.

☐ Some cavalrymen rode their horses so rigorously that they grew additional bone in their backsides and thighs. The added stress of prolonged physical activity causes the bone to grow heavier and stronger. On the other hand, lack of physical activity results in bone loss. Astronauts, after long space voyages, show an alarming loss of bone.

☐ The only bone that does not connect with any other in the body is the hyoid bone, which is in your throat and supports your tongue and its muscles.

☐ The largest and also the strongest bone in the body is the femur or thigh bone. The smallest is the stirrup bone, one of three little bones in the middle ear.

☐ Modern research indicates that, in the future, electrical current may be used to regenerate bone growth. In other words, if a person loses an arm, he may be able to grow another.

☐ Your backbone is not one bone but twenty-six all linked together like a chain.

☐ We have as many vertebrae in our necks as a giraffe, though of course the giraffe's are much longer.

☐ Some people were afraid of the first X rays because they believed their bodies could be seen right through their clothes.

☐ The first Olympic stadium in Greece was based on the size of Hercules' foot. Six hundred of these, at approximately 31.75 centimetres each, or a total of 190.5 metres, established the length of the stadium.

☐ There was no junk food in Herculaneum, the ancient Roman city that was buried in hot lava in A.D. 79 after Mount Vesuvius erupted. According to experts who studied the skeletons of the victims, most skeletons – including those of two octogenarians – had all their teeth.

☐ A prisoner in a German jail, serving a six-year sentence for robbery, used his teeth to escape. He gnawed away at the wooden bars of his cell until he could squeeze out. Alas, although he chewed his way to freedom, he was caught and put in jail again – this time behind iron bars.

☐ Boys usually get their first milk-tooth three weeks before girls get theirs.

☐ Some adults never grow their four wisdom teeth, many others have to have them removed because the gums or mouth are not big enough to accommodate them.

☐ The patron saint of toothache is St Apollonia. She is depicted in paintings holding a tooth or forceps in her hand.

☐ Teeth have been transplanted, but they fall out after a few years.

3

Outer Coverings

☐ If you had no skin, your body would dry up like a prune.

☐ Your skin weighs almost twice as much as your brain.

☐ It takes 200,000 frowns to produce one wrinkle.

☐ The thickest skin on our bodies is found on the soles of our feet.

☐ We have about three million sweat glands in our skin, which if stretched out and placed end to end would cover a distance of 30 miles.

☐ The skin of a woman, laid out flat, would cover about 1.58 square metres. A pregnant woman's skin would cover 1.72 square metres.

☐ The ridges in your fingerprints help you to hold on to things.

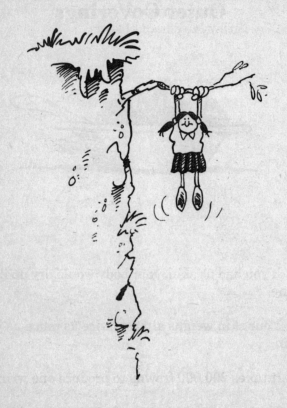

☐ The foot is a much more sensitive thermometer than the hand.

☐ Billions of bits of skin flake off your body every day.

☐ During the time of witch trials in the Middle Ages, birthmarks were considered to be marks made by the devil – a sure sign of a witch.

☐ A three-month-old foetus already has a distinctive set of fingerprints.

☐ Chinese businessmen in the third century BC used fingerprints as personal seals.

this is my personal seal!

..and this is mine!

☐ No two sets of fingerprints are alike; even identical twins have different fingerprints.

☐ Our toenails grow about four times slower than our fingernails.

☐ Your fingernails are made of the same substance as feathers, claws, beaks, quills, and horns.

☐ Fingernails have been transplanted successfully.

☐ If you never trimmed your fingernails, they would be nearly 4 metres long by the time you were eighty years old.

☐ The longest fingernail belongs to Shridhar Chillal. His thumbnail was recently measured at 101.6 cm.

☐ The hair of an elderly Indian monk was nearly 8 metres long when he died in 1949.

☐ The nails of the hand you write with grow slower than those of your other hand. The fastest growing nail is on the middle finger.

☐ Nails grow much slower in arctic climates than in warm ones.

☐ Goose pimples are the places where hairs used to be. In days when humans were a lot hairier, the body's response to cold was that the hairs stood on end. The hairs created a trap for air, which acted as an insulating blanket against the cold. Now, with humans growing less hairy, all that happens is the initial response of the body, and little bumps rise where hairs used to be.

☐ Your hair grows a total of 2,500 centimetres a day. Each hair grows .025 centimetres daily, and there are 100,000 hairs on your head.

I'll have .025 centimetres off each hair, please!

☐ Cutting or shaving your hair does not make it grow any faster or any slower.

☐ A man could grow about 8 metres of whiskers in his lifetime. Shaving them off would take him about 3,336 hours, or 139 days.

☐ From earliest times all over the world people have been superstitious about the cutting of hair and nails as it was believed that they were part of the soul. In some European countries it used to be considered very unlucky for a child's nails to be cut before his or her first birthday, while in Uganda a baby was never to have his hair cut before he had received a name. When hair or nails had to be cut it was important that it was burnt or hidden so that it would not fall into the hands of wicked sorcerers.

☐ Hair is dead. Hair follicles, or roots, are alive, and they push dead cells up through the scalp. This dead stuff is what you comb, brush, plait, and corn-row.

☐ A human hair can support a weight of 79.38 grams. A rope made of 1,000 would support you and three friends. If it were made of 2,000 hairs, it could support three full-grown men.

☐ The longest beard ever measured and recorded was that of a Norwegian man, Hans Langseth, born in 1846, who emigrated to the United States. His beard was 5.33 metres long when he died in 1927. It is now in the Smithsonian Institution in Washington, DC.

☐ When Peter the Great, czar of Russia, could not grow a beard, he outlawed beards throughout his kingdom.

☐ We lose approximately fifty hairs from our heads each day.

☐ When a hair falls from your head a new one will not grow out of the same follicle for three months.

☐ Your hair grows faster in the morning than at any other time of day.

☐ A scab is really clotted blood that forms a kind of net over a cut. This mass of dried blood cells protects you while new skin is being made. When the new skin is ready, the scab drops off.

☐ Some of the best-preserved mummies in history, found in bogs in Denmark, were about 2,000 years old and so well preserved that local police were able to take the mummies' fingerprints.

☐ After the age of twenty, a person stops getting new freckles.

I'll have three million of them by then!!

4

Beneath the Surface

☐ A person living in a hot climate can sweat as much as 13½ litres a day.

☐ A human being is 60 per cent water. Losing one-tenth of that amount can be fatal. You can lose far more blood – nearly 3½ litres – and live.

☐ The average person expels about 1.14 litres of gas each day.

☐ Astronauts wear air-conditioned underwear. Their space suits get pretty warm, since they are designed to hold in body heat. So when the body needs cooling, cool water is piped through tubes in the underwear.

☐ You wash your eyes every time you blink. Your tears are antiseptic and kill germs.

☐ We blink about twenty-four times a minute, that is twenty-two more times than a cat or a dog.

☐ One of the earliest studies on the digestive system was made by a doctor who examined a living stomach through an open window caused by a gunshot. A youth stationed at Fort Mackinac, an army post occupied by US troops after the American Civil War of 1812, shot himself by accident. The hole that was made in his stomach remained as he recovered, and his physician took the opportunity to study the inner workings of the stomach, looking in daily and making notes. The doctor later published a book on his findings.

☐ Mountain man Jedediah Smith saved the lives of two members of a trapping party in South Dakota who had fainted from loss of water. He buried them in sand up to their necks to keep their bodies from drying out, then went to find a water hole, filled his canteen, and returned to revive the dying men.

☐ The average person eats 1.36 kilos of food a day, or 497.13 kilos a year, or the equivalent of three whole elephants in a lifetime.

☐ Your lungs are lightweight enough to float on water.

☐ Your body is being renewed constantly. In one year, 98 per cent of the atoms in your body will be replaced by other atoms.

☐ It takes thirteen muscles in your leg and twenty in your foot to turn your foot outwards. You use seventy-two muscles just to speak one word.

☐ The exercise that the average adult gives his muscles each day is equivalent to loading 10,886 kilos from the ground on to a one metre high shelf.

☐ Harry Houdini, probably the best escape artist the world has known, attributed his success to his well-trained muscles. By holding his breath for long periods, and by expanding and contracting his various muscles, there was no situation from which Houdini could not escape – including locks, hand-cuffs, chains, straitjackets, and sealed trunks under water.

☐ A human being in bare feet leaves such a strong scent in his footprints that it is possible for another person to follow his trail.

☐ There are about two hundred and fifty thousand million traces of sweat left in a footprint.

☐ A runner in a 90 metre dash needs nearly 8 litres of oxygen. There is only about a litre available in your blood, so fast breathing has to supply the rest.

☐ If the three million or so minute air sacs or alveoli in your lungs were levelled out, they would cover an area the size of a tennis court.

☐ The left half of your heart is much stronger and better developed than the right half. That is because the left half has to pump blood through your entire body, while the right half only has to pump blood through the lungs.

☐ You can't sneeze with your eyes open.

☐ The highest recorded sneeze speed is more than 100 miles per hour – the speed of a cork shooting out of a champagne bottle.

☐ Aristotle, the ancient Greek philosopher and scientist, believed that the liver was the seat of the emotions.

☐ When we stand up, if we didn't have valves in our veins, all the blood in our bodies would pour down, filling up our legs and feet.

☐ Although your heart weighs only about one hundredth of your body weight, it uses one twentieth of the blood supply that flows through your body.

☐ Your heart rests between beats. If you add up the length of time of these rests over a lifetime, you will find that your heart stands still for about twenty years.

☐ You cannot hear a heartbeat. The sound you hear when you listen to someone's heart is that of the valves of the heart closing. The beat itself is a silent contraction of the muscles.

☐ Your heart beats seventy-two times every minute. By the time you are sixty-five years old, your heart will have beaten about 2½ billion times.

....eighty nine million, four hundred and sixty three thousand, two hundred and ninety six....

stop fooling about!
.. start it up again!

☐ Certain people in India are able to control their own heartbeats. They can actually make their hearts stop for short periods of time.

☐ The pressure of blood rushing through an artery has enough force to lift a column of blood one and a half metres in the air.

☐ It takes about twenty-three seconds for blood to circulate through the entire body.

☐ In the seventeenth century when the first blood transfusions were made by drawing the blood from one man's veins and putting it into another's, people wondered whether the character of the person receiving the blood would be altered. For instance, would the behaviour of a violent criminal improve if he were given the blood of a devout man?

☐ The tiniest blood vessels, or capillaries, are fifty times thinner than the finest human hair.

☐ Placed end to end, the blood vessels in a human being would stretch 70,000 miles, or almost three times around the equator.

☐ The knockout in the boxing ring happens when a boxer is struck a powerful blow that causes a chain reaction in his circulatory system. This ultimately causes the supply of blood in the heart, lungs, and brain to pool in the abdomen, and to decrease the circulation in the brain, resulting in a loss of consciousness.

☐ A person who is eleven kilos overweight has over 5,000 extra miles of blood vessels through which the heart must pump blood.

☐ Inside your body, your blood is blue. It turns red only when it mixes with oxygen, which is what happens when you cut yourself and bleed.

☐ Every second, your body manufactures 2½ million new red blood cells. Within a month, all your red blood cells are replaced with new ones.

☐ A single blood cell makes about 3,000 round trips through the circulatory system.

☐ The Egyptians thought so highly of the heart that they did not remove it from a corpse, as they did the other internal organs, but mummified it along with the rest of the body.

☐ A dog's nose is about a million times more sensitive than a human's.

☐ Hiccups are even faster than sneezes and blinks.

☐ Unlike the cough or the sneeze, which do important jobs for the body, scientists are not sure what a hiccup is for.

☐ The mouth produces nearly a litre of saliva each day, but a lot less during the night. As saliva helps protect the teeth and gums against bacterial infection and decay, if you only cleaned your teeth once a day it would be better to clean them before bedtime than in the morning.

☐ Spit is useful. Your teeth grind up what you eat and mix it with spit so that the food can slide down your throat easily.

☐ There is enough phosphorus in the human body to make 2,000 match tips.

☐ Zinc in the human body is an essential ingredient, but it can prove fatal if a person is bitten by a rattlesnake. Then the zinc interacts in the bloodstream with a protein in the rattlesnake venom, poisoning the victim.

☐ Humans should rust, just like frying pans and bicycles, when iron and oxygen in the body meet. Fortunately, we have a neat built-in rustproofing system. Iron in the body is swallowed up by ferritin balls, which act as storage bins for waste iron until it is needed to make new red blood cells. Then it is released only a few atoms at a time, giving it no chance to rust.

could you give her a look over?...she's going a bit rusty!

JOE'S GARAGE

☐ The iron in a human being could make one small nail.

☐ Your small intestine is four to five times as long as you are.

☐ We have about 50 miles of nerves in our bodies.

☐ Nerves take four to six weeks to regenerate themselves.

☐ Muscle strength varies at different times of the day and night. Your handgrip is strongest at six in the evening and weakest at three in the morning.

☐ Studies show that since a person starts to feel better as soon as he starts crying, all tears are tears of joy.

☐ We blink more often when we are tired, bored, angry, embarrassed or under pressure. We blink less often when we are reading. Moreover, the more difficult the text we are reading the less we will blink.

☐ If you try to stop blinking for about three or four minutes you will blink more often than your normal rate immediately afterwards.

☐ You cannot burp when you are lying on your back.

all right! all right! you can EXHALE it now!

☐ The average human being inhales 15,900 litres of air a day.

5

A Good Head on Your Shoulders

☐ It takes about one fiftieth of a second for a pain in your big toe to reach your brain.

☐ Your brain, more complex than any computer, operates on about the same amount of power that would light a 10-watt bulb.

☐ The human brain weighs about 1.36 kilos. If all the water was squeezed out of it, it would weigh around 283 grams.

☐ The only cells in the body that are not replaced are the brain cells. The supply you have now must last you the rest of your life.

☐ The human brain can remember approximately 50,000 smells.

☐ Our brains stop growing when we are about fifteen years old.

☐ The twentieth president of the United States, James A. Garfield, could write classical Greek with his left hand and Latin with his right – at the same time.

☐ In Siamese twins, one twin is generally right-handed and the other left-handed.

☐ Around 10 per cent of boys are left handed. For some reason, the figure is lower for girls.

☐ Dr Truman Stafford, a Harvard instructor at the age of twenty, was asked to do an amazing feat of maths in his head – to square an eighteen-digit number. The stress was so great for him as he struggled for the answer that he spun around the room, pulled his trousers up over the top of his boots, bit his hand, and rolled his eyes before he answered – correctly.

☐ The Kerr clan of Scotland, whose members were mostly left-handed, built their castles with outer staircases that spiralled up anticlockwise so that they could fend off swordsmen with a left-handed parry as they backed up the steps.

☐ By the time you are ten years old, one side of your brain is dominant. If your left brain is dominant, you will be right-handed. If the right side of your brain is dominant, you will be left-handed.

☐ The highest frequency that adult humans can hear is about 20,000 cycles per second. Children can hear frequencies up to 40,000 cycles.

☐ The lowest frequency that humans can hear is 16 cycles per second. If we heard anything lower than that, we'd hear the sound of our muscles working.

☐ You get dizzy when you spin around because there is liquid in your inner ear that spins around with you. When you stop, the liquid keeps spinning, giving you a dizzy sensation.

☐ The first hearing aids, which improved hearing by about 20 decibels, were shaped like trumpets and held to the ear.

☐ Some identical twins are so alike that they can wear each other's contact lenses.

☐ Only one out of three people in the world has perfect 20-20 vision.

☐ The human brain can remember approximately 50,000 smells.

☐ Eight per cent of males are colour blind. Far fewer females are affected.

☐ The human eye is so sharp that if you stand on the top of a hill on a clear and moonless night you can see a match being struck 50 miles away.

☐ On the inside corner of your eye is the remnant of a third eyelid. Some animals still have this protective lid, which closes from the centre outwards.

☐ In a glass display case in the Boys' and Girls' Room of the Omaha Public Library, there is a human scalp, attached to wavy blond hair with a reddish tint. The scalp was donated by William Thompson, a Union Pacific telegraph operator. On August 6, 1867, Thompson was ambushed by Cheyenne Indians, shot, and scalped. The sensation of the knife on his scalp woke him up, and he grabbed the scalp from the startled Indian and ran. The warrior did not follow him.

☐ When Danish astronomer Tycho Brahe lost the tip of his nose in a duel, his vanity ruled, and he had it replaced with a gold one.

that's a nice nose!
..did you pick it
yourself?

☐ An ordinary nose can distinguish from 4,000 to 10,000 different smells. The nose of an expert in the perfume business might develop enough sensitivity to distinguish 30,000 different scents.

Ah yes... number 29,642... essence of skunk and loganberry...

☐ If you were given a piece of apple and then a piece of potato both of the same shape and size while your nose was held and your eyes blindfolded, you probably would not be able to tell which was which.

☐ The only letter sounds you can make without your tongue are *m, p, h, f,* and *v.*

☐ Each of the tiny little bumps on your tongue contains about 250 taste buds. Each taste bud can taste only one flavour – sweet, salty, sour, or bitter.

☐ You can't taste anything solid unless part of it can be dissolved in the saliva on your tongue.

☐ Mountain climbers experience a loss of appetite and a loss of weight at altitudes above 3000 metres. It is known that water is lost from the lungs in the very dry mountain air which reduces body weight, but nobody can explain why taste becomes duller.

☐ Your tongue is the most movable organ in your body. It can move in every direction because it has plenty of muscles and no bone.

☐ According to some experts, noses are adapted to do a particular engineering job in their native regions. In hot, dry places like Egypt, long noses moisturize the air along lengthy passages. In humid climates like Kenya, where there is no need for extra moisture, there are short, flat noses. In cold places like Finland, long narrow noses warm the air on its way in.

THAT COMPOSER'S GOT NO NOSE!

....Really? how does he smell?

...AWFUL!

cheek!

☐ Eighteenth-century Czech composer Josef Myslivecek, had no nose. It was removed by a doctor who told him the removal would cure him of a disease.

☐ There are over 650 muscles in our bodies. They make up 30 to 50 per cent of our body weight.

☐ When we smile we use seventeen muscles.

6

Beginnings and Endings

☐ The largest newborn infant of recent times was an 11.04 kilo baby boy born in Turkey.

☐ Every human being once spent about half an hour as a single cell.

☐ On January 8, 1910, a nine-year-old boy and an eight-year-old girl of Amoy, China, became the parents of a normal baby boy. They were the youngest set of parents ever known.

☐ The king of Siam had fathered 370 children by the time he died in 1910.

☐ More babies are born in early spring than at any other time of year. September is the next most frequent time for births.

☐ An Australian mother gave birth to twins so far apart that one was born in December 1952, and the other in February 1953.

☐ A woman in Russia bore sixty-nine children. In all, there were sixteen pairs of twins, seven sets of triplets, and four sets of quadruplets.

☐ The smallest full-grown female humans on the planet Earth, the Pygmy women of Africa, bear the largest babies in the human race, averaging more than 3.85 kilos at birth.

☐ One out of every ninety births results in twins.

☐ On average twins are born nineteen days earlier than single babies.

☐ To hasten childbirth, some American Indian tribes used to place an expectant mother in open ground and have a horseman gallop straight at her. The rider would avoid her at the last moment but it was hoped that the fright he caused would induce the woman to give birth.

☐ At birth human brains are not much larger than the brains of most baby apes.

☐ The youngest mother in the world, a Peruvian Indian, was only five years old when she gave birth in 1939 to a healthy 2.6 kilo baby boy. They later attended school together.

☐ An ancient Indian manual on childbirth recommended that a baby should be delivered with the assistance of four old and wise women whose nails were well trimmed. Why, the book did not say.

☐ To keep their bones straight, newly-born babies were once wrapped up, or swaddled, from their heads to their toes in bandages. It might have been as long as a year before the baby was finally free from his cocoon-like wrap.

☐ The first incubator was a crude aquariumlike device developed by an unorthodox young Parisian obstetrician to save a patient's premature baby. Soon he was in demand for other cases, but it was very expensive to give such special care. To solve his financial problems and still save the babies, he put the infants on display at fairs, charging the eager crowds an admission price to watch them as they were fed, bathed, and had their nappies changed.

☐ Quadruplets occur once in every 512,000 births. Identical quadruplets occur once in sixteen million births.

☐ A girl will reach three quarters of her adult height when she is seven and a half years old. A boy will not reach his until he is nine.

☐ The oldest American was said to be Charlie Smith, a former slave who was born in 1842 and died in 1979. At sixty-five, Charlie Smith was starting a new job picking fruit in an orchard. When he was one hundred and thirty-six, his seventy-three-year-old son came to visit him in a convalescent home.

not so fast, you young whippersnapper!!

☐ The 1662 English *Book of Common Prayer* says that 'the days of our age are threescore years and ten', or seventy. It is only now, over three hundred years later, that average human life expectancy in England has matched this figure. At the time, life expectancy was only about thirty-two.

☐ Two hundred years ago, nearly half of all women died before their thirty-fifth birthday.

☐ By the year 2000, one third of the population will be over the age of sixty.

☐ About 2,500 people in the Soviet Union are believed to be well into their hundreds. At the age of one hundred and sixty-eight, Shirali Mislimov of Azerbaijan, USSR, was still walking half a mile a day and working a few hours in his garden. He said one of the tips for a long life was not getting married until he was sixty-five.

☐ The average life span of a caveman was eighteen years.

☐ Some scientists believe that humans have the potential to live around 150 years.

☐ In the late seventeenth century, a one-hundred and fifty-two-year-old man was discovered living simply in the English countryside. He was brought to London and presented to the king, given employment in a noble household, and plied with plenty of food and drink. In a short time, he died – of an overly rich diet.

☐ Body-snatching was a common practice in nineteenth-century Scotland. Medical students were always in need of new bodies to dissect to study anatomy, and the most likely place to get these was from newly dug graves. Relatives sometimes hired professional grave watchers to protect the graves of loved ones.

☐ Medical schools paid a flat fee for an adult's corpse and paid by the inch – about 2½ centimetres – for a child's body.

☐ Philosopher Jeremy Bentham ordered in his will that after he died his body be used for medical study and, when that was done, that the skeleton be re-assembled on wires for anatomy lessons. Also in his will was a requirement that his head be mummified and stuck on top of the skeleton, and that the whole thing be presented at each meeting of Bentham's organisation. To this day, Bentham's skeleton is rolled out at meetings of the Utilitarians – a group that proposes practical solutions for problems.

☐ Mrs Martin Van Butchell's will stated that her husband would inherit her fortune as long as he met certain conditions of her will, including a provision that she be kept above ground. To get around these awkward terms, Butchell embalmed his wife, dressed her up, sat her in the parlour, and even had the public come in to view her as he enjoyed his new wealth.

☐ The headhunting Jivaro of South America have a complex method of preserving and shrinking the heads of their enemies. No one knows for sure why these shrunken heads remain so well preserved, but it is believed that the Jivaro use a secret ingredient – the juice of a plant called *huito* in the process of boiling the head.

☐ A rare modern-day mummy is the body of Lenin, former political leader of the Soviet Union, which has been preserved and put on display for the public since his death in 1924. The government will not give away the secret of how the body was preserved.

☐ So many people wanted to see the first cremation of a human body in America, in 1876, that a huge hall had to be rented for the service, seating 1,500 people.

7

Bugs in the System

☐ Louis Pasteur, the famed scientist, carried a portable microscope with him, tucked under his coat, to see if the food served at friends' homes was safe to eat.

☐ Laughing sickness, or kuru, a rare disease that affects only the Fore tribe of New Guinea, is 100 per cent fatal. Until recently, the Fores were cannibals, and scientists believe that the virus for the disease may have been spread by eating brain tissue.

☐ Queen Elizabeth I stuffed her mouth with cloth when she appeared in public because her face had sunk in from the loss of her front teeth.

☐ In the eighteenth century, a noblewoman died from regularly painting her face with white lead.

☐ Certain sounds in the English language are real germ spreaders, particularly the sounds of *f, p, t, d,* and *s.*

☐ Tapeworms can grow to 9.75 metres long inside the human intestine.

☐ The most contagious disease in the world is the common cold. You can catch a cold from someone who sneezed in a room he had left up to 30 minutes before.

☐ Queen Victoria of England, later learned to be a carrier of the blood disease haemophilia, spread the disease through just about every royal house in Europe. This is because her children, inheritors of the disease, married into other royal families.

☐ In the Middle Ages, it was believed that leprosy could be spread through the breath as well as through physical contact. Lepers were required by law to stand downwind if they stopped to speak to anyone on a road.

☐ Scientists have new evidence to support the theory that the Roman Empire fell because its people went mad. It seems that the citizens of Herculaneum stored their wine in lead vessels and drank water that flowed through lead pipes, which could have caused mental disabilities.

eat!...drink!... and go completely... ...mad!

☐ Stone Age human fossils show evidence that our early ancestors suffered some of the same complaints of the body as people today, such as rheumatoid arthritis.

☐ Soldiers have keeled over in a dead faint during inspection. It seems the tension of standing rigidly straight can be so great that not enough blood fills the heart, resulting in a lowering of blood pressure and a blackout.

☐ Girls of well-to-do families in eighteenth-century Europe often had greenish complexions. Experts say the eerie malady was the result of delicate foods, tight corsets, lack of ventilation, and little exercise.

☐ A person is most likely to suffer a heart attack at nine in the morning and least likely to have one at nine in the evening.

☐ Statistics show that a person's health can be impaired following a major life change in his or her regular routine. The death of a close family member is rated 63 on a scale from 1 to 100. The beginning of school rates a 26, and even Christmas rates a 12.

death of a close family member	63
personal injury or illness	53
addition of a new family member	39
death of a close friend	36
beginning of school	26
a change in schools	20
Christmas	12

☐ A ninety-year-old man in Iowa has been hiccuping since 1922, 10 to 40 times a minute, and is still at it as of this writing. There is no scientific explanation for this, but the man says the hiccups started when he tried to lift a 158 kilo hog.

☐ The hiccups of a young man admitted to an English hospital in 1769 were heard half a mile away.

☐ A workman in New England, trying to remove an unexploded charge of dynamite, set off an explosion that sent an iron crowbar through his skull. The crowbar was removed, with no apparent harm done to the man, although, afterwards, people who knew him said his gentle manner was gone and that he was prone to severe outbursts of bad temper.

☐ Moses stuttered. So did the philosopher Aristotle, the storyteller Aesop, and the orator Demosthenes. Demosthenes used to stand on the seashore with pebbles under his tongue and shout above the roar of the waves, claiming that this cured his stuttering.

☐ The highest recorded decibel level for a human snore is 69, almost the level of a pneumatic drill. Winston Churchill reached 35 decibels.

☐ It is estimated that 35 million Americans snore while they sleep. Some experts believe that snoring began with the cavemen, who made terrifying noises in their sleep to frighten away savage beasts.

☐ It is thought to be better to be a sensitive sneezer as germs are blown out before they have a chance to get into the body. Eskimos and other inhabitants of very cold climates suffer fewer respiratory infections yet are frequent sneezers.

☐ Influenza epidemics are sometimes very severe. It has been claimed that more people died in the 1918 epidemic than in the Great War which preceded it.

☐ While colds and influenza are more likely to happen in winter, common childhood diseases like mumps and chicken-pox are more likely to occur in summer.

☐ The word quarantine is based on an Italian word meaning forty days, the favoured biblical timespan for a period of isolation.

☐ One taste of the death cup, the world's deadliest mushroom, is fatal. As soon as its poisons enter the bloodstream, there is nothing that can be done. The mushroom contains five deadly poisons known to man, one of which is a hundred times as strong as cyanide.

☐ During the Great Plague of London the houses of infected people were marked with a red cross and the words 'Lord Have Mercy On Us'. Also, a fire was lit at every sixth home to help purify the air.

☐ A few rare human beings are born with a visible tail. Everyone has a tailbone, but usually it is hidden beneath the surface.

☐ Twenty per cent of the population sneeze when they move into a bright light.

8

Healings and Dealings

☐ There is proof that Stone Age people performed surgical operations, sawing off limbs with tools hand-made of stone or bone. One skull, found in south-western England, shows that the patient was operated on – and also that he died before recovering.

☐ Powdered mummy was once an important ingredient in European medicine. When the supply of mummies dwindled, 'new' mummies were made from recent corpses.

☐ The Aztec Indians began eating arsenic regularly as children, to build up their immunity to the poison.

☐ Egyptians mixed a concoction of hippopotamus fat and mouldy bread crumbs to use as a medicine – and it worked. Some say it was a forerunner of penicillin – which was developed from mould.

☐ The Chinese paid their doctors for keeping them well but stopped paying them if they became sick.

☐ The first medical specialists were found in ancient Egypt. A sick person sent a description of his ailment to a temple of health, and the priest there sent out a physician skilled in the treatment of that condition. Surgery was sometimes performed, including the removal of stones from the bladder, cataract operations, and amputations.

☐ In ancient Babylon, doctors exhibited their most desperately ill patients in the public square, hoping that anyone passing by who knew of a remedy would speak up.

OK- I've applied the gunpowder, so don't chew anything made of metal or your head will explode!!

☐ In colonial days, one of the cures for toothache was 'brimstone and gunpowder compounded with butter' rubbed on to the gums.

☐ It was once commonly believed that a horse chestnut carried in the pocket prevented rheumatism.

☐ A surgeon's favourite hobby, sailing, helped him to cure one of his patients, who had a severe curve in her spine. The doctor implanted a device fashioned after the one that helped keep the sails trim on his boat. This gadget held the patient's muscles taut so that the spine straightened.

☐ In 1595, Queen Elizabeth I's royal physician prescribed a mixture of powdered 'muck, amber, gold, pearl, and unicorn's horns' to relieve the British ambassador's constipation.

☐ Hippocrates (460–377 BC), the father of medicine, is said to have set fire to a library when he was young – so that nobody would know what he knew.

☐ In seventeenth-century England, the local barber was also the local surgeon. The same brass basin that caught lather during a shave was used to catch the blood spilling from patients.

and what would you like today?.. ..a haircut or a major operation?

☐ One folk remedy for hiccups is to cover your head with a wastepaper basket and have somebody beat on it. Another is to drink nine swallows of water from your grandfather's cup without taking a breath. Still another is to spit on a rock, then turn it over. Or you can wet a piece of red thread with your tongue, stick it to your forehead, and look at it.

☐ Before anaesthesia was discovered, a surgeon established his reputation by the speed with which he could operate. Famous surgeon Robert Liston is said to have cut off his assistant's fingers in his hurry to get the job done.

☐ Whooping cough was once treated by putting a live frog in the patient's mouth.

☐ It has been established that having a pet can help lower the owner's blood pressure.

that should cure your headache – if it doesn't we'll add a few slugs!

☐ In the eighteenth and nineteenth centuries, leeches, sluglike creatures that suck the blood, were used to treat the sick. Several leeches were applied to the affected part of a sick person's body – in a ring around the head, for example, to cure a headache. Leeches are still sometimes used by boxers, after a fight, to treat a black eye.

☐ One Roman physician cured headaches and gout with an electric fish.

☐ In modern India there is a hospital that is said to treat digestive complaints with various types of crushed jewels, such as powdered emeralds for liver trouble.

☐ In one culture, where modesty prohibits the display of the body, doctors may make available small figurines of a naked body which allow the patient to point to the afflicted part without removing any clothing.

☐ A crude method of inoculation began in the seventeenth century with the Chinese, who discovered that they could build resistance to smallpox by pulverizing the scabs of a smallpox victim and inhaling it through the nostrils.

☐ Horseradish was used at one time to treat complaints ranging from scurvy to baldness.

☐ In Britain in the nineteenth century it was thought blue glass helped cure diseases. The patient was told to lie in the sun under a blue glass screen.

☐ A doctor may now ask a heart patient to swallow the stethoscope. There is one instrument that is only 2½ centimetres long and, once inside the body, transmits the sounds of the patient's heart to a microphone for the doctor to hear.

☐ Some people were afraid of the first vaccinations, which were derived from cows. They were afraid that their vaccinated children might behave like cows.

☐ Sofie Herzog, a pioneer doctor in Texas, removed so many bullets from gun-fighting cowboys that she made a necklace of them, which she wore throughout her life. The necklace was buried with her.

☐ Pegleg Smith, a mountain man, was trapping beaver when an Indian bullet smashed his leg. He wrapped a buckskin tourniquet around his thigh and amputated the leg below with a hunting knife. He whittled a leg out of hickory wood for himself, which he later pulled off and used as a weapon when he got into brawls.

☐ From the reign of Edward the Confessor in the eleventh century until that of Queen Anne in the early eighteenth century, it was believed in England that a disease called scrofula, which attacks the glands of the neck, could be cured by the touch of the king's hand. The disease was aptly named 'the King's Evil'.

☐ The Turks of ancient Anatolia fed cooked bird tongues to children who were slow in learning to talk.

☐ Since the early days of medicine there have been bogus doctors – or quacks as they came to be called – promoting miracle cures for diseases and other illnesses. If the quack could not identify what was wrong with a patient he would invent a diagnosis. The patient might have been told he was suffering from such obscure conditions as Glimmering of the Gizzard, Hocklegrockles, Quavering of the Kidneys or Wambling Trot. And for every condition the quack had a remedy that he would make sure the patient purchased, such as Vatican Pills, Tincture of the Sun, Pilula Salutiferens or Great Cordial Antidote.

☐ It was not just individuals who were fooled or persuaded into buying the quack's remedies. In the early nineteenth century, the state of New York paid a large sum of money for the formula of a remedy for hydrophobia. The remedy was a mixture that included the ground-up jawbone of a dog, the crushed false tongue of a newly-foaled colt and the green mould from an English coin of the reign of George I.

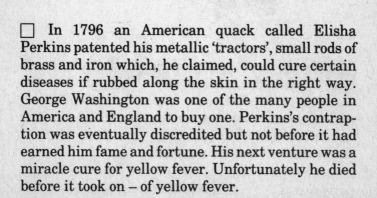

☐ In 1796 an American quack called Elisha Perkins patented his metallic 'tractors', small rods of brass and iron which, he claimed, could cure certain diseases if rubbed along the skin in the right way. George Washington was one of the many people in America and England to buy one. Perkins's contraption was eventually discredited but not before it had earned him fame and fortune. His next venture was a miracle cure for yellow fever. Unfortunately he died before it took on – of yellow fever.

☐ A nineteenth-century Scottish physician, Dr Shortt, was certain that hiccups were caused by a disorderly nerve and that they could be cured by the application of a heated instrument along the nerve's path in the back and neck. It is doubtful that many patients were willing to endure burns and blisters to solve their hiccuping problem. It was a clear case of the remedy being worse than the illness.

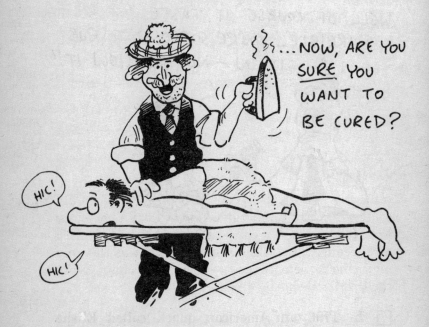

☐ Old proverbs show that people did not always have much faith in their doctors. They said that 'the doctor is more often to be feared than the disease', that 'if you have a physician for your friend, tip your hat and send him to your enemy', and even that 'one doctor makes work for another'.

9

☐ Beliefs and Curiosities

☐ Francesco A. Lentini, known as the three-legged wonder, was born with three fully developed legs. He could walk, run, jump, ride a bicycle, ride a horse, ice skate, drive his own car, and kick a soccer ball with all three legs. Lentini boasted that he was the only man who came equipped with his own chair, using the third and shortest leg as a stool.

☐ In 1770, Parliament declared a marriage would be null and void if a woman had used artificial devices to seduce a man into marriage. Artificial teeth, wigs, and even high-heeled shoes were considered fraudulent.

☐ On the Sandwich Islands, chiefs were once accompanied by servants carrying portable spittoons. It was believed that if they could capture some of their enemy's saliva they would be able to bewitch him.

☐ People once believed that the mucus which flows down your nose when you have a cold was the brain leaking.

☐ Bronze Age people used drugs for illness but not to repair the body. They were used mainly to chase away the evil spirits that inhabited the body, causing the ailment.

☐ Peter Stuyvesant, governor of colonial New York, lost his leg during a battle on a Caribbean island in 1644. The leg was amputated, given a Christian burial, and accorded full military honours. Meanwhile, the rest of Stuyvesant went on to live another twenty-eight years.

☐ Mayan Indians sharpened their teeth to points, drilled holes in them, and stuck them full of jewels.

☐ The British once believed that it would take a frecklefaced king to conquer the Welsh.

☐ Queen Elizabeth I set a new style when she took a bath every month, and others soon followed the practice.

☐ In eighteenth-century Scotland, citizens sometimes gathered at an execution to collect the criminal's blood, which was believed to cure various diseases.

☐ Frederick the Great of Prussia hated water and almost never washed his hands or face. Instead, he painted his cheeks each morning with red paint to look fresh and healthy.

☐ Soap, invented by the Sumerians in 3000 BC, was not adopted by Europeans for cleaning the body until the Middle Ages. Before that, it was used only for laundering clothes.

☐ Anne Boleyn, second wife of Henry VIII, had an extra finger on her left hand.

☐ It is believed in some primitive cultures that a person's spirit enters and leaves the body through the mouth. Therefore, a well-meaning friend might try to keep the spirit from leaving by holding the dying person's mouth and nose closed.

☐ A person in Japan is more likely to ask your blood type than your astrological sign. Employers are even showing preference to certain employees because of their blood types.

☐ People once thought that a sneeze was a sign that death was near, so they started saying 'God bless you' as a kind of condolence for what might be a last *achoo*.

☐ A Hindu fakir of Bengal, India, extended his right arm above his head in 1902 and kept it that way to show his contempt for, and mastery over, pain. He never took his arm down, even when a bird built its nest in the fakir's open palm. When he died, he was buried with his arm extended.

☐ It was once believed that a vein ran from the third finger of the left hand to the heart, which is how the wedding ring came to be worn on that finger.

☐ In the 1800s, people went to phrenologists to have the bumps on their heads read. Queen Victoria even sent her children to a phrenologist. The idea was that bumps indicated a particularly strong area of the brain indicating the person's special abilities.

Of course it's an unusual set of bumps!... I just fell down your stairs!

☐ On the American frontier, there was a folk remedy for every complaint. To rid oneself of birthmarks, for example, it was necessary to rub them with the hand of a corpse or the head of a live eel three mornings in a row. A frontiersman in the northern forests would fasten the right eye of a wolf inside his right sleeve to ward off ills.

☐ A farmer near Trier, West Germany, sells licks from his cow to bald people because some people believe that the cow's tongue stimulates the naked scalp, helping to make hair grow.

☐ Siamese twins Chang and Eng Bunker, who were born joined at the hip in 1811, grew up, married a pair of English sisters, fathered a total of twenty-two children, and died within two hours of each other in 1874.

☐ In medieval times, if a man's eyebrows touched each other, that man was believed to be a werewolf.

☐ Women in the Middle Ages used the poisonous juice of the belladonna plant to enlarge the pupils of their eyes, believing that would make them appear more beautiful.

☐ The horn of a unicorn was once thought to have miraculous curative powers, especially as an antidote to poison, and the horns were sold for enormous amounts of money. But as unicorns do not exist, except in fables and myths, the much coveted horns were more likely to have been from an elephant or narwhal whale.

☐ An old proverb says that when the sun rises the disease will abate. The proverb is based on the Old Testament story of Abraham, who wore a precious stone with healing powers around his neck. When Abraham died it is said that God placed the stone in the sun.

☐ Queen Elizabeth I wore what was reputed to be a magic locket around her neck to keep her free from infection.

☐ The popular English children's nursery rhyme 'Ring a ring o'roses' has its origins in the plague-ridden Middle Ages. The ring referred to one of the dreaded symptoms of the disease, the ring rash, the sneezing symbolised illness and death, and the line 'All fall down' meant all fall dead.

☐ Until recently people were very sensitive about draughts from windows or doorways as the old proverb 'if cold wind reaches you through a hole, say your prayers, and mind your soul' illustrates.

☐ Frederic Chopin, the famous composer, was so afraid of being buried alive that he asked his friends to cut open his body before they buried him. His friends obliged, and Chopin's heart was sent to his native Poland.

☐ The Empress Marie-Louise of France could fold her ears.

☐ Queen Anne employed tailors and tinkers to treat her worsening eyesight.

☐ Julius Caesar and Napoleon Bonaparte were both born with a tooth already through, and the French king Louis XIV was said to have been born with two.

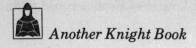
Another Knight Book

Alan Brown

FIRST CLASS

A book of batty beginnings.

Did you know

* that the first teabags were invented by mistake?
* that until the nineteenth century it was illegal to have a bath in Spain?
* that the first lady to wear a swimsuit was arrested for indecent exposure?
* that one of the first cures for toothache was to eat a mouse?

Find out all about these and hundreds more batty beginnings in FIRST CLASS – packed with fascinating and freaky facts to amuse and amaze.